To my wonderful nephews

# Soul Food for the Whole Family

## Easy Stress Management Techniques for Children and Parents

### Learn How to Meditate with the Meditating Manatee and the Dancing Dolphin

Copyright © 2023 by Alina Olteanu

# Foreword

This delightful booklet is extremely timing, arriving at a time when millions of parents and children are experiencing unparalleled levels of unhealthy and dangerous stress.

Having a simple and powerful tool like meditation, can change the lives of parents, children, and families.

Dr Olteanu's use of a conversation between two friends, the Meditating Manatee and the Dancing Dolphin, makes learning about how to meditate, fun and easy for parents and children.

~Dr Sandy Gluckman, PhD, Learning and Behavior Specialist

# Table of Contents

- Introduction for Parents          9

## Two Simple Meditation Techniques ......................... 13

- Sitting Meditation                14
- Breathing Meditation              15

## Stress Management for Children ........................... 17

## Meditations for Children ..................................... 23

- Sitting Meditation                25
- Mantra Meditation                 27
- Moving Meditation                 29
- Mindfulness Meditation            31
- Visualizating Meditation          33
- The Practice Of Meditation        35

# Introduction for Parents

Nutrition, sleep, and exercise are the main pillars of health, but one of the most important ones, and often neglected, is stress management. Chronic stress, even in children, is the root cause of many health problems.

In today's world, children and teenagers are hearing the word "stress" often but do they know what it really means? Do parents know what stress is and how it affects children?

Stress got a bad reputation but it's not intrinsically bad, it is actually the body's reaction to keeping us alive. Stress is dangerous mainly when it becomes chronic, when the body doesn't get a chance to relax.

When we're under stress, the body reacts in two main ways, a reaction that is called "fight or flight". If the reaction is short and the body return to baselines fairly quickly, stress didn't cause any harm. However, if the body reacts to stress for prolonged periods of time and it doesn't know how to return to a more relaxed baseline, stress can plant the seeds of chronic illnesses.

There are many stress management and mind-body techniques for children and their parents.

Here is a list of just a few techniques that parents can learn and practice with their children. Sometimes parents need the guidance of a healthcare professionals but there are also many free online resources.

- Meditation
- Mindfulness
- Yoga
- Progressive muscle relaxation
- Guided imagery
- Biofeedback
- Massage
- Music therapy

## How Meditation Works

Meditation works as a stress management tool by switching off the "fight or flight" stress response and allowing the body to switch on the relaxation response.

When children meditate, they become less reactive to stress. Meditation changes the chemistry of stress. Instead of making more stress hormones, like cortisol or adrenaline, the body and the brain work together harmoniously to make different molecules and neurochemicals that trigger a relaxation response.

There are different types of meditations: sitting meditations, breathing meditation, mantra meditation,

walking meditation, guided meditation, mindfulness meditation.

In most types of meditations, the mind needs a point of focus. It's a myth that we can stop our mind from having thoughts, but we can give it a point of focus, like the breath or a word, so that it goes beyond thoughts.

Meditation is not a religious practice; however, every spiritual tradition in the world has developed some form of meditation to discipline the mind.

## Make meditation a family practice

I suggest to parents to experiment with different types of meditations until they find one that works for them and their children.

In order for children to meditate or start practicing a mind-body stress management technique, parents have to practice it as well. As adults, we can't expect children to meditate if we don't. If we want children to meditate, the parents need to learn how to meditate first.

There are two basic meditation techniques that are easy to learn and can set the foundation for a daily meditation practice for parents and children: sitting meditation and breathing meditation.

# SITTING Meditation

Find a quiet spot in the house, where you can sit comfortably

No distractions like pets, phones, iPads, TV, computers

Sit quietly for few seconds or minutes, breathing normally, with your eyes closed

Take one, slow deep belly breath through your nose — hold for 4 seconds — breath out through your nose slowly.

Repeat 3 times

# BREATHING Meditation

Start with the "sitting" meditation (see previous instructions) and continue to focus your attention on the breath flowing in and out, effortlessly, without trying to change it.

You can repeat "breathing in/breathing out" quietly in your mind.

If you start noticing thoughts or have any feelings in your body or hear sounds in the environment, gently release them and focus again on your breath

Start with 10 minutes/day, twice a day, increase slowly to 20- 30 minutes, twice a day

# Stress Management for Children

**Meet the** Meditating Manatee **and the** Dancing Dolphin, **two friends in the vast ocean who are supporting each other to feel happier at school and at home.**

Meditating Manatee **just returned from a meditation retreat with her mom and is teaching her friend, the** Dancing Dolphin **how to manage his stress.**

**He has been having difficulties focusing in class and has difficulties sleeping because he worries so much about his grades.**

**He is also so nervous before his violin concerts and baseball game that he feels like throwing up.**

**He wants to quit orchestra and stop playing sports, because it doesn't feel fun anymore.**

Meditating Manatee **and** Dancing Dolphin **have decided to meet after school every day to figure out how to deal with stress.**

Meditating Manatee: I've heard that you want to quit baseball and violin because it's too stressful!

My mom told me that meditation can help us deal with stress better.

Do you want to learn how to meditate?

Dancing Dolphin: Absolutely! However, what do you think happens when I feel stressed at school all the time?

Do you think it is bad for me?

Meditating Manatee: Did you know that reacting to stress is not always bad? It can actually keeps us safe and alive.

When the brain thinks there is a danger, it creates the kind of chemistry that will either help us fight the danger or run away from it. This is called the "fight or flight" response.

What makes it bad for our health is if it never turns off.

If we are constantly in "fight or flight," after awhile, we start getting sick.

That's why it is so important to learn how to manage our stress every single day!

Meditating Manatee: Hello my friend! Last week we talked about stress. Are you ready to learn how to manage stress through meditation?

Dancing Dolphin: Sure but... What is meditation and how can it help me feel less stressed?

Meditating Manatee: Meditation is to the brain what working-out is to the body. It is a brain exercise that helps your mind.

When we meditate, we become less reactive to stress.

Meditation changes the chemistry of stress. Instead of making more stress hormones, like cortisol or adrenaline, which are not good for you, your body and your brain are starting to work together to make healthier molecules that help you relax. Isn't that awesome?

These are some benefits of meditation:

- Helps you feel more calm and relaxed
- Allows you to be more creative.
- Have more confidence and will be more comfortable with who you are.
- Might have more energy and be focused when studying.
- May feel more love and the desire to express love.
- Life seems to become more effortless and joyful.

Let's learn how to meditate today! Are you ready?

Dancing Dolphin: Yes! After I learned that meditation has so many benefits, I can't wait to get started!

Meditating Manatee: The same way we can practice different sports for our physical health, we can practice different kinds of meditations for our brain health: sitting meditations, breathing meditation, mantra meditation, walking meditation, guided meditation, mindfulness meditation, to name just a few.

# SITTING Meditation

Meditating Manatee: Today, let's start with a very simple sitting meditation

Find a quiet spot in the house, where you can sit comfortably:

- **No distractions like pets, phones, iPads, TV, computers**
- **Sit quietly for few seconds or minutes, breathing normally, with your eyes closed**
- **Take one, slow deep belly breath through your nose — hold for 4 seconds — breath out through your nose slowly.**
- **Repeat 3-10 times**

Do this for a week and next time we meet let's talk about how it worked for you.

**One week later, our two friends meet again.**

Meditating Manatee: So how do you feel after practicing the sitting meditation for a week?

Dancing Dolphin: I have noticed that I am sleeping better and I don't get upset so easily anymore!

# "SO HUM" MANTRA Meditation

Meditating Manatee: Today let's add to the sitting meditation and learn a new kind of meditation that uses a sound as a point of focus for the mind.

This sound is called a "mantra" and the one we're going to learn today is called "so hum" mantra meditation

- Start with the "sitting" meditation (see instructions from last week) then start repeating quietly, in your mind, the mantra/words "SO HUM"
- Repeat the words slowly, gently, effortlessly
- If you start noticing thoughts or have any feelings in your body or hear sounds in the environment, gently release them and focus again on the mantra "SO HUM"
- Start with 10 minutes/day, twice a day, increase slowly to 20- 30 minutes, twice a day

# MOVING Meditation

Meditation can be practiced everywhere and it doesn't have to be sitting!

Dancing Dolphin: That sounds like fun! I love moving and dancing!

Meditating Manatee: Let's practice a moving meditation together.

- Focus on your heart center, in the middle of the chest
- Start breathing in and out slowly
- Recall a positive emotion or think of something or someone you love
- Start moving (swimming/walking) while focusing on your heart center, breathing in and out slowly, while repeating phrases like "I am peace", "I am happy", "I am relaxed", "I am joy".

# MINDFULNESS Meditation

Meditating Manatee: Meditation can involve all of our senses!

Dancing Dolphin: That's mindfulness meditation, right?

Meditating Manatee: Yes! Let's practice a mindfulness meditation together

Use daily or as needed, in a stressful, tense situation

- Take a deep breath in and slowly breath out
- Notice and name silently 3 things that you hear in your environment
- Notice and name silently 3 things that you can see
- Notice and name silently 3 things that you can touch
- Notice and name silently 3 things that you can taste or smell
- Restart your regular activity; repeat as needed, several times throughout the day

# VISUALIZING Meditation

Dancing Dolphin: I sometimes can't sleep, especially the night before a test or my violin recital.

Meditating Manatee: This is a meditation that you can do before going to sleep, the night before an important test.

In your bed, before falling asleep:

- Breath in through your nose to the count of 4
- Hold your breath to the count of 4
- Breath out through your mouth to the count of 4
- Repeat 4 times
- As your drifting to sleep, imagine how wonderful you're going to feel when you're going to successfully pass your test or how much you're going to love playing the violin!

# The Practice of Meditation

Meditating Manatee: Over the past few weeks, you learned a breathing technique, a sitting, a mantra, a moving meditation and a mindfulness meditation.

Do you have any questions so far?

Dancing Dolphin: I love meditating every day and it makes me feel so good but how do I know if I'm meditating correctly?

Meditating Manatee: There is no wrong meditation. Sitting with your eyes closed, with the intention to meditate, focusing on your breath or a sound, that is a meditation.

If your mind wanders, as it often does, gently let go of any thoughts, and return to your point of focus, your breath or a mantra.

It is called the "practice of meditation" because every meditation you do is a new experience and you have to keep practicing every day.

# About the Author

Alina Olteanu, MD, PhD is the founder of "Whole Child Texas", a pediatric integrative and functional medicine practice in Frisco, Texas. She believes in treating the whole child, spirit-body-brain. Dr Olteanu can be reached at www.wholechildtexas.com

# 31. FAITH

*"And without faith it is impossible to please God, because anyone who comes to Him must believe that He exists and that He rewards those who earnestly seek Him." Hebrews 11:6 (NIV)*

*"For we live by faith, not by sight." 2 Corinthians 5:7 (NIV)*

❉ ❉ ❉

**Faith:** *complete trust or confidence in someone or something.*

I remember as a little girl, my Dad having us memorize Hebrews 11:6 and explaining those words. In order to please God I had to live a life of faith. I have never forgotten this verse and all that it has meant to me thru the years of my life. I'm reminded of it each time I hear my middle name, Faith, too. What a beautiful reminder that is.

God requires faith from you, but not a complex faith, a simple one. He wants you to fully trust Him with every area of your life. Are you willing to give it all over to Him and choose to live a life of faith? It's not easy and can even be scary at times, but the reward is incomparable.

God asked much faith of me in 2019 when my husband took a new job and we moved our family to another state. There were times I felt like I was walking in the dark but God was always there, making my faith in Him even stronger.

This little devotional book is the outcome of stepping out in obedient faith to what God put on my heart.

**Practice The Word:**
How can you show greater FAITH today in God's plans?

**Study Deeper:**
Hebrews 11.

# ABOUT THE AUTHOR

## Precious Mast

My husband Jonathan and I are followers of Jesus who are passionate about living on mission as disciples of Jesus Christ. One of our favorite things is studying the truth of God's word together and learning how we can apply it to our lives. We have four beautiful kids and love to spend time together as a family, kayaking, enjoying bonfires, hiking, and hanging out at the beach. We also enjoy having friends over to the house, drinking coffee and talking about life and the Lord. Our passion is to see every single person transformed and mobilized by Jesus and living out their God-given purpose for His glory.

Made in the USA
Middletown, DE
11 June 2021